Sp   -

MW00834424

Souls:

An
Anthology of
Poems

Austie M. Baird
-Editor, Cover Artist-

Austie M. Baird is a born and raised Oregonian, holding both History and Education degrees from Eastern Oregon University. She is continually inspired by the beauty of the world around her and uplifted by the overwhelming love of her family. Long before becoming a wife and mother, Baird connected with the power of the written work, finding healing properties in both reading and writing. She draws strength from the power words have to make dreams realities.

A.B.Baird Publishing
Oregon, USA

Printed in the United States of America

First Printing, 2018

ISBN 978-1949321036

Cover Art Image by Austie M. Baird

A.B.Baird Publishing
66548 Highway 203
La Grande OR, 97850
USA

www.abbairdpublishing.com

Table of Contents

Table of Contents

Dedications

There are some people in this world who deserve their names in lights, but for now, ink on paper will have to do: for Mum, Dad, Annie, Neil, Trudy, Ethan, and my delightfully mad grandparents. Thank you all for everything.
- Maya Elphick-

For all those who feel alone in their struggle. And for the brightest light in my life, my little sister Taylor.
-M.R.S.-

I dedicate my work to my beautiful daughters, E and A. You are rainbows after the storm.
-L.M. Steel-

To Rogelio, the framer of my words.
-Heini Talip-

To anyone who has ever felt like the darkness has won - remember that we are all made of stardust.
-Eloise-

To those I am blessed to call friends- your strengths supplement my own, your lights illuminate my dark, and your laughter lightens my load- thank you for loving me!
-Austie M. Baird-

To our readers,

As we assembled the works in this anthology, we felt like there was a greater story to be told than that of 8 authors who understand mental health struggles.

We saw the story of us all: the story of the person who thinks they have conquered their demons, only to find themselves staring back into the face of those monsters yet again. We saw the journey through the depths of inner destruction, when things are so dark that finding your way out feels nearly impossible. We saw the story of daring to hope: the moment when the first glimmer of possibility for better days is first spotted. And we saw redemption: not for anything but for ones self- the moment when demons have been made friends and the darkness is made to be a beautiful part of the soul that serves to display the brightness of future dreams.

We invite you to join us on this journey- our journey- as we travel through the darkest of times together hand in hand in search of better days.

From our souls to yours, thank you and remember- you are not alone.

Love,

Splintered Souls

Night Blossom

She's in that dark-hearted,
just-started mood.
Weeds growing from the roots of her hair
and so many dead flowers
bleeding beneath her fingernails,
red polish and
petal speckled shoes
from all the lovers she's doubted.
Black lipsticked baby
in tinted glasses
and a rose tattoo on her shoulder.
Thorns stuck between her teeth
like the remnants of a stubborn dream,
she licks her wounds clean.
There's a darkness in the air tonight
and yet she wears blue jeans.

- Maya Elphick-

Grey Space

For a week,
I have waited for
the morning fog to clear,
a cardigan-covered hand
grasping a coffee mug,
the other outstretched
towards the grey space
between love and hate,
light and dark...

-Eloise-

Offering

I float on my back
in the lake where
my monster lives,
arms outstretched and palms
facing the sky –
an offering.
My ears are filled
with a silence
that only water can give,
my eyes wandering to
the back of my head –
where the world is an
upside down place
that looks far more beautiful
than this one...

-Eloise-

Lost Boy - Lost Girl

I play with Peter Pan's shadow,
the darkness flitting to
all corners of the room,
silhouetted in the bright
of the night light.
My mind has manifested
into an outline of a person
who doesn't want to grow up -
when the emptiness
pulls her right back in.
I spend the early morning hours
sewing the shadow
back against my limbs,
cool to the touch.
At night, I let her
run wild like the darkness...

-Eloise-

Nocturnal Self -Survival

The weight of the world
held in sweaty palms
clenched tight
to bed sheets
and racing
age-old thoughts,
aching for release
from relentless
suffocating darkness.

Trenches dug
in the mattress.
Repetitive rooting
by nails dirty
from exhuming
old wounds.
Lost memories and
wrong words
in the deep
of night.
Regrets scrape
sharp echoes
across my heart.

Mountains of pain
moved in the mind
with hand held
trowels, scratching
the surface
piece-by-piece
one peak then another.
Dusk til dawn.
bone breaking work.
Body finally gives way
to exhaustion
with the rising sun.

Oh how heavy it feels.
All this work of nocturnal
self-survival.

-A. Brown-

Doubt

Despite my best efforts
You keep returning
to me,
Like a dark
Unwelcomed
Homing pigeon

Landing your
Unease
Deep in
My open heart
And making
There
A nest
Of complications.

Your cooing
Song of
Masochist
Thoughts
Ever draws
Me in
The message rolled
And wrapped
To your bony leg
Reads

"Doubt"

Feels like home
Feels like hell

But...

Despite my best efforts

You return

Again

And again

And again.

-A. Brown-

I Cannot Bind it All in Stone

Is it not enough
that each morning
I dig a hole
to the center of
my heart,
clear away the
debilitating debris
of doubt and fear
from the broken night
and fill in the deep
void with heavy,
placating plaster?

Mortar that hardens
that same heart
from feeling each
numbing moment
after the breaking
dawn that breaks

me down,
step after familiar step.
The leaden gypsum is
strenuous and rough
in my tender fleshy cavity.

Oh how it weighs me down.

What more could be

asked of me?
I cannot cement
one more part
away from who
I am.
I cannot bind
it all in stone.

> - I would sink into the depths of me.

-A. Brown

The Binding

some days, I question
how I have grown to love
the things that bind me.

this bittersweet stockholm
syndrome,

the careful way in which
I am held & kept by the world.

it clipped my wings &
I barely bled,
barely bled.

so tell me, am I
grounded yet?

-Emily Adams-Aucoin-

Gradually

these things happen gradually:
sunlight filling the hours,
fattening them with light.

I used to know them all by name.
by what opens to them.
but that has faded like aging vision.
gradual, like shadows falling
over our kitchen-
we used to love better here.

unopened bills lay fanned
on the marble where we once spread
soft butter on bread,
praising the ease.

gradual, the way you hung black
blankets one by one as makeshift
curtains to block the morning,

this that intrudes &demands gravely.

gradual, the way love comes to some
bit by bit, sacred accumulation.
&the way it leaves others.
like the moon, &how
the waxing carries the waning.

you stand by the bedroom door
with your hand on the switch
&curse the darkness. we do not see
the irony.

-Emily Adams-Aucoin-

How to Stay

I am stitched together with
moderate care, & each morning,

weights must be placed
on my body so that I don't
float away:

bills, a career,

I was told *this is how
you stay.*

none of this feels right,
or like how it's supposed to be,

but I suppose we're all grasping
something,
trying not to leave.

I stay indoors these days &
praise the ceiling for how it
keeps me.

-Emily Adams-Aucoin-

Primetime

the television offers us tragedy
&we can't stop watching.
we can't stop watching.

children die in our living room
&the remote is a privilege.
the remote is a privilege.

we mourn through commercials
&hold each other tighter,

whisper words that sound nothing
like war.

-*Emily Adams-Aucoin*-

The Cost

we do not know when, exactly,
the money will be gone, only
that it will be.

only that as of right now, we have
five hundred dollars in a bank
account that must pay for:

rent- the wall & roof that keep
us,

health insurance- for fear that
these bodies will betray us,

medical bills- for when they
inevitably do,

& student loans- because we must
do *something* to contribute.

we drive with the gaslight on
& our fingers crossed,
wondering often & gravely
if it will always be this much
of a struggle to exist.

if we will always live in fear of
the cost.

-Emily Adams-Aucoin-

My Voice

my voice is a thing underused.
less neglected than muzzled,
it sits restless in the back of my throat
&wants, pacing.

a domesticated thing.

it is let out seldomly,
&only under controlled conditions.

I am not lacking in good intent,
keeping restraint like this. I prune
so that beautiful words bloom.

I pluck away the sharpness,
the low-hanging fruit.

some nights, it all threatens to slip
through my teeth.
&some nights, my tongue becomes
weaponry. &my throat rattles with all
that I do not say.

but I clench my jaw until it's done.
& I don't hurt anyone.
I don't hurt anyone.

-*Emily Adams-Aucion*-

Reflection

i avoid them the best i can
instead i admire my feet, supporting my entire being
my legs, walking me wherever i need to be
my hands, helping me in all my day's work
my chest, reminding me of my femininity
my neck, supporting my head so it may think and sense
my lips, speaking true and encouraging words
my shoulders, taking on more than i ever thought possible
but staring at my reflection, i avoid meeting my eyes
for though they are a beautiful hazel brown
they see with such judgement and hate
the second we meet again, my eyes are filled with disgust
they cannot seem to see the miracles my body is capable of
only the flaws
when i catch a glimpse of them i shut them tight
listen to my head and my heart instead
silence my eyes, you're seeing too loudly.

-M.R.S.-

Worth More

you're fat, he said
not an insult but a fact
yes i am fat
with wide hips and thick thighs
i'm working on loving this body
to everyone's surprise
his lips said "fat"
but his delivery said
inferior, disgusting, incapable of loving
taking up too much space
worth determined by the size of my waist

-M.R.S.-

You've Hidden Yourself

i watched you eliminate
every other person
there was only him
you weren't you anymore
you were only the you he fabricated
but i couldn't tell you
because the you i could have told
the you that would have listened
was nowhere to be found
i don't even know if you know
where you're hiding
so it's just him
and a shadow of you

-M.R.S.-

Mr. Anxiety Visits

he sits in my head like a splinter
a sharp piece of wood attacking my mind
he taunts me for he knows the meticulous care
it will take for me to remove him
every inch of my being works to tweeze him out of my brain
but he kicks his feet up
as i inadvertently welcome his stay
and his stay is always longer than expected
he doesn't leave often, but when he does
he'll almost always return again
a loyal customer indeed

-M.R.S.-

Flower Child

doubting the love of another
is her mind's greatest burden
she wanders through fields
plucking the petals
of love me love me not's
until the fields are bare
and love has nowhere left to blossom

-M.R.S.-

Silent Sorrow

there's not much left to be said
let's just sit here in silence instead
silence drowns out sorrow eventually
you hear it echo if you listen intently
soon the echoes become hums
the humming becomes peaceful for some
yes, there are lucky ones
who grow used to the hums
and flourish amidst turmoil

-M.R.S.-

There's Nothing

what if i just let it all go
trusted the pain
surrendered myself to it
let it become me
consume me
maybe i'd be better off
perhaps feeling pain
is better than feeling
nothing at all

-M.R.S.-

Call Her By Her Name

she's a shape shifter, a temptress
she's your kryptonite
she's captivating, she's cunning
she's present but out of sight

she comes around often
most welcomed when you're weak
she's a leech, a lamprey
you can hide but she shall seek

you attempt to make her leave
try declaring her eviction
but she's a stubborn constant
and her name is addiction

-M.R.S.-

Addiction Treads Water

so i hid from her under the dock that day
watching her gracefully walk away from me
i thought she had finally escaped
she breathed in the horizon
hoping for no more encounters
but it didn't take long
before she was searching for me
looking to reel in her addiction
we locked eyes, i smiled
i knew i won her over again
she tossed a life jacket my way
even though in her heart of hearts
she wanted me to drown

-M. R.S.-

Old Habits

Secret feelings dwell,
In deep dark corners:
Urges seeped in shame:
(to heal by hurting,

To blot the emotional wrench with a physical sting,
To swig down the burn until my head is whirring fuzz
And all thoughts become a distant haze,
To lay there and let a type of love ruin me so that hurt
Sweats into the mattress and out of me)

It is so hard to be normal
On the outside,
When under constant ambush on the inside,
By Old Habits,
Bigger than me.

-L. M. Steel-

Minefield

My mind-map brain, it's a scatter graph of musings,
Links as tenuous as fireflies and ash,
It's a minefield to meander around: so many fault-lines and
grenades in waiting,
Each wondering is an exertion: exhausted wandering without
compass points, just aching joints.
How lonely it is to be so lost in my own head,
Stood in the middle of an infinite loft space, littered with half-
open boxes, accompanied only by the mosquito alarms of every
corner,
This fight or flight existence is wasted on the untrained and
wingless,
But there are no marked exits anyway

-L. M. Steel

Welcome Into My Heart

Welcome into my heart
Where pain has limbs
To trample
over self-belief:
Where it pivots
on pride,
And trounces
on triumphs.

Welcome into my heart,
Poisoned against itself,
Ever since the monster
Fed me a script
I scribed on my wrist.

Well Come
I ache for
Better company.

-L. M. Steel

What Kind?

What kind of masochism is this
that wraps itself around my joints
and leaves me this dis
jointed
That makes me dig my nails so deep into this feeling,
Rooting myself there like a great oak into the earth,
Gripped white knuckles into leather, braced for the
impact of metal on metal.
Was I born with it?
Or did I grow it-
When I sipped on the sap of the Sadists,
Digging around in their darkness with futile, fruitless faith,
Naive and hungry for some small seed of kindness I
could pour love on,
to grow in my own bones?
But instead, all that grew was this acquired taste,
this unquenchable desire for distraction or
destruction and the increasing inability to know the
difference.
What kind of masochism is this?

-L. M. Steel

<u>*Slipping*</u>

Slipping since Six,
On ice and sticks,
This world is a dangerous place.

Slipping under spells,
Into bad crowds,
Away from safety,
Into arms on slippery shoulders

Slipping between sheets,
Out of negligees,
Into the eyes and lies that
Let things slip in.

Slipping out of halos,
Off of pedestals,
Beneath radars
And expectations

Slipping on wet floors,
Tear-drenched, blood-soaked
Surfaces:
Scars slowly surfacing

Slipping away,
Further from self,
Never having mastered
How to stay steady for long

-*L. M. Steel*-

Glass Heart

Such a young fool
In an ageing body,
To believe hurt will just settle
Like dust,
As if I do not feel everything:
Heart full of embers
A sea could not cool,
As if my skin is not a map
Of old pain from old flames,

So naïve to pretend
I am not glass.

Foolish girl
To think
Fragility will not
Break me
From the inside
Out, where everyone
Will see
Eventually

-L. M. Steel

Highly Strung

Highly strung
Loosely
By a fraying thread — that is
Unravelling,

Tangled in
Knots, so easily undone
With careless words.

One utterance
And everything
Will fall down.

-L. M. Steel

Concrete Rose

Cursed by
pessimistic petals,
blessed with
tomorrows thorns,

I bloomed wrong
and wilted correctly
on the sidewalk
of sad soles.

-Heini Talip-

Then and Now

In the beginning,

    b r e a t h l e s s

I was shiny and
happiness was mine.

Now,

    s u f f o c a t i n g

memories of my umbilical cord
hang me in the dark.

-Heini Talip-

Depression, I Think

The emptiness came back today.
My body died in bed and told my bones to follow.
My eyes blinded themselves
with paper cranes.

I feel so hollow
like an old oak rotting from the inside out,
bark carved crudely with the names of those who've ventured
inside.
I'm finding it hard to cough up these words.
Can't find the energy to rhyme,
can't find time at all.
I just want to sleep
or drown myself in the bath.

I can see my optimism trodden into the carpet
and I can't pick up the pieces
leaving me to stare up at the ceiling
and the blackness between the stars.

I thought I'd killed this,
I thought it was buried in the garden
with the dead pets

but now I see it again
sitting across from me
at the dining table.

- Maya Elphick-

Senescence

Minutes in pockets,
brushing up against my palms
as I feel around for time,
never satisfied.
Appetite for hours
becomes hunger for weeks,
I cry as the days wash away
and yet I oversleep.

- *Maya Elphick*

A Small Rebellion

There is a place,
it's just beyond the glass and forever,
where little metal people
tap their sharp, tin fingers,
slowly rolling cigarettes
and flicking the ash into my fishbowl brain.
I grow tired of swimming in circles.

They lick salt off their teeth
and poison my water
as I rock
rock
rock
the bowl
and splash my poetry onto their shoes.

- *Maya Elphick*

A Mess

She fell through the cracks
between the words on pages.
Flowers and thorns and bloody messes,
crime scenes torn out from spines
of books her father almost read to her.

- *Maya Elphick*

Story From Suburbia

You fell apart
and into the bottle
while he poured drinks
for those glued-up girls
in your favourite bar.

- Maya Elphick-

Not Enough, Never Enough, Too Much For Someone

red lips
never red enough
too pale, too frail
for the boy
who kisses
like a sport

long legs
not long enough
too lumpy, too bumpy
to shave without
drawing blood
from skin
and staining bathtubs

sick mind
too sick to love
too busy, too dizzy
caught up in
her daily hurricane
they can see
the storm
on her lips

never enough
too fragile, too tough
too much for everyone
too little for everyone else
too confident
too shy
too hard on herself

- Maya Elphick-

Ink

I wrote poetry on paper
while she wrote help on her arm.

There's a difference between us
and we have the scars to prove it.

- *Maya Elphick*

Intoxicated

My personality is of an
insecure drunk.

I'm just stumbling around
hoping you don't regret me.

- *Maya Elphick*

The Film

Don't ask why I can't love you.
I have pushed the answer through my lips
time and time again.
I am sore from spitting out divorces and affairs
I have watched play out
like black and white film.
Ask my mother,
ask my father,
ask my sister and all her blunt-tongued lovers,
ask my friends who tie hearts to train tracks
but don't ask me.
After watching so many plane crashes
the sky screams pain.
You will not fool me with your wings.

- *Maya Elphick*

Not Quite

I'm not quite glass
because I'm not quite see-through,
I'll just trick you
and pick you apart
like not-quite-glass people do.

- Maya Elphick-

Numb

There was a time when snowfall meant
running outside in pyjamas so thin,
my body wrote poetry on them at night.
My bare feet skimmed the white, shattered glass
as a dance broke free from my shivers
and you laughed from the window
at someone you didn't understand.

Now it means something different.
The snow seems so distant,
a stranger now you aren't here
to laugh at me
and hold my blue feet at midnight.

- Maya Elphick-

Bitten

You say,
my mind
is like a pop-up book
you wish you'd never opened.

Conjuring words
that catch heartbeats
and dreams,
pinning them to pages
hoping they won't bleed
monochrome.

.   Did no one warn you
about books and covers?
I'm a folded up
paper cut
waiting to happen.
But you never do listen
when I say
my mind is dark:
it sleeps in ink
not rose water.

But please feel free,
flick through me
and gulp and gasp,
it won't be the first time
this book bites back.

Don't flatter yourself,
I have scars from bigger men than you.
You can find them on page 15.

- *Maya Elphick*

The Cocoon and The Chrysalis

I have moths in my stomach,
not butterflies,
never butterflies.
They're far too pristine and pretty
to mix with the likes of my insides.

Capture and cage the dark-winged things
with white light,
artificial and fake,
hanging from the branch of a candy cane,
sickly sweet and sticky
like pink lip-sticked kisses
making words flutter like

butterflies.
Nervous eyes
upon a pale blue sky,
rhyming rhymes to comfort myself.
"Give 'em hell, give 'em hell, give 'em hell"
is what the moths want to say
but moths don't talk
and no butterfly would dare speak for me
through chapped lips.
No chapel cares for what I have to say
and the confessional is never vacant anyway,
always
full of butterflies,
fucking butterflies
and their beautiful, fucking wings.

- Maya Elphick-

Cut Outs

You are on the tip of my tongue,
you are each word spoken:
sentences stringing like rope around my neck.

Your face is found on every cover
of every self-help,
3 steps
to forgetting book.

You sit by my bedside at night,
you're the scratch in my clothes
and the nightmares
nightmares,
creaks on the stairs,
you stare at me with my father's eyes.

Take your hands off my life,
I left you behind.
I want to cut you out of me
and out of my mouth,
my books,
my bed,
my dreams.

I want to leave you where you left me.

- *Maya Elphick*

Hungover

vodka spilled
from the shattered glass
upon her bedside table
falling onto the letter
she wrote the night before
a letter she couldn't salvage
a truth she'd never send
there was no courage anyway
red eyes
unrest
unwell

-M.R.S.-

Toy Top

she was spinning in ovals
not in circles, never perfect circles
perhaps calling them ovals
is presumptuous still
figure eights isn't even right, no
she asks me to stop mapping her action
for she refuses to live in patterns
she only spins

-M.R.S.

Thoughts at Bay

there's this chaos about her
if you painted a picture of her thoughts
you'd paint a hundred ships lost at sea
they'd battle the storms
but struggle without anchors

-M.R.S-

Shield

numbness
set across her skin
a protective layer
made of broken promises
and no one could touch her
even if she let them

-M.R.S.-

Empty

how is it possible
to feel such nothingness
and still breathe
as a something

-M.R.S.-

Absent

tingling feet
trembling fingers
knees give out
mind grows weak
and then there's nothing
so you sit in nothingness
while numbness sets in
a split second thought
is it nothing you're after
or is nothing after you?

-M.R.S.-

Stuck in a Rut

they stand up above
peering into the darkness
calling to me
offering ropes and ladders
lanterns and harnesses
even with a tool, i fear
i cannot make that climb
not on my own
i need someone
but i can't let anyone
risk getting stuck
in this pit with me

-M.R.S.-

Dream Demons

they're circling me
setting secrets free
i cannot hear them
overwhelming mayhem
circling faster all the while
each wearing sly smiles
alas they're mere illusions
only my own delusions
the terror escapes
but first I must scream

-M.R.S.-

Are You Emotional?

i go crazy
trying to convince myself i'm not crazy
my skin's often lifted
goosebumps all over
i cry when i laugh
and I freeze when I talk
so yes, to answer your question

-M. R. S.-

Summer Storm

My depression comes like a summer storm,
heat lightning rising from my fingertips.
The accompanying clap of thunder
is too far for anyone to notice.
The rain has not stopped for two weeks –
April showers in early June.
There will never be enough metaphors
about the sky to describe how I've forgotten

what the color blue looks like some days...

-Eloise-

Tourist

She feels like a tourist
in her own mind,
taking mental snapshots
for the scrapbook
her lucid dreams
could never piece together...

-Eloise-

Windowpane

Standing on her tiptoes,
a ballerina brushing the tears
off the window pane,
baby palms
pressed against
the cold glass.
The rain clouds
know where the

darkness lives...

-Eloise-

Damaged Goods

The porcelain claw foot tub
cradles my damaged goods,
washing away the dirt and grime
of past mistakes gone terribly wrong.
I let my head sink below the water,

bubbles rising to the surface...

-Eloise-

Best Friend

Anxiety is not a good friend,
but she is my best friend,
always there to push together
the broken pieces with
the edge of her foot.

We plan vacations,
and she compiles a list
of horrible things that
could happen if we went,
so we sit at home in pjs instead,
sipping coffee in my reading room
while she talks a mile a minute -
drawing me in.

I often say, "I'm fine,"
and she is the only one
who doesn't believe me,
a smirk on her lips...

-Eloise-

Pennies

Depression tastes like
cracked pennies,
eucalyptus,
and Dove soap,
wearing flannels
in the dead of Carolina summer
because your skin feels cold
to the touch...

-Eloise-

Drowning

Remember what it's like
when the tears come,
when the hollow in your chest
houses a girl whose head
is barely above water,

a place for drowning...

-Eloise-

Friends with Benefits

My depression likes to
hang out at night,
like a friend with benefits
that texted you they were
coming over - already in the driveway.
He kisses me at the door
before saying hello,
ready to give a smirk
and a cigarette at a

moment's notice...

-Eloise-

Drunk Girl

I write poems to the drunk girl
sitting on her hands at 1:30
in the morning,
the one who put alcohol
to her lips
just to feel something...

-Eloise-

Brain on Fire

I can't write when my brain is on fire.
Panic leans back in a reclining chair,
sipping tea and waiting out the flames.
I want all my memories back in the right
filing cabinet, not scattered on the floor
waiting to be swept up by a janitor never hired.
My mind has smoke alarms for these days,
but all the doors are labeled without exit signs.

Panic runs to the heart when she gets too warm.
My ribs rattle under the pressure
of an untamed heart.
She beats against the cage, begging to be free...

-Eloise-

Suitcase

My suitcase is full
of bottled up feelings
too big for TSA,
and I am asked
to pour them into
the black-lined trash bins
next to the metal detector -
a device that can scan me
for bombs but not for pain -
my hands raised above my head,
a sign of surrender...

-Eloise-

My Mother Says I Take Too Many Mental Health Days

I wish I could tell my anxiety
That my mother named her
Sadness instead -
inform Anxiety that
she had an eviction notice
and she is a few years overdue -
that she is just a figment
of a "sad" girl's imagination.

-Eloise-

Spoken For

You said if I wasn't already spoken for,
you would have asked me on a date.
I replied with a blue Powerade
at your door when morning came
because I've seen the same hangover
in my own eyes and the sharp laugh
four vodkas deep when you joke
about seeing a therapist.

I am taken, but never spoken for.
If we ever get the chance,
I hope to one day tell you about
all the things I've never said...

-Eloise-

Anxiety Brand Clothing

I want to take off my thoughts
like anxiety-brand clothing,
and bare my soul to you...

-Eloise-

Familiar

He kissed me straight on the mouth.
"What do they taste like?" I asked.
"Hmm?"
"The broken places."
I expected him to say -
Smoke. Lemon drops. Intoxication.
"Familiar."

-Eloise-

Welcome

Welcome to my heart,
wipe your feet here,
on the mat of melancholy.

Watch your step,
It's dim here,

chilly too.

Find a seat, mind the dust.

It echoes, I know.

Never furnished this place,
Not even for myself.

-Heini Talip-

Suffering Scenery

Landscape of my soul:

A wing abused sky
over
petal bruised Earth.

-*Heini Talip*-

Breaking

I am this
biology of bubbles,
pulse
without purpose,
wine glass flesh
dreaming
of breaking.

-*Heini Talip*-

Weak

This fire in me
is just inconsolable incense,
these tears
the pH level of worthless,
my hands
either cups or boulders,
this heart
injured by its own ignition.

-*Heini Talip*-

Sad Spine

In this portrait of my particles,
I frame my breath like a puddle,
my sad spine
is a doodle
never meant to be art.

-*Heini Talip*-

Barrel of a Gun

I have in me
the loneliness of a tree,
adoring the sun,
the barrel of a gun
my world
is pointing at me.

-*Heini Talip*-

Sad Things

Roads to nowhere,
snowflake suicides,
memories we lose like dandruff.

Candle lights begging
darkness to blow them,
clouds polishing space.

Sad things
in a sad world,
how could it be anything else?

-*Heini Talip*-

Six Words

I share
a dandelion's despair:

Breaking.

-*Heini Talip*-

Raven Shaped Sorrows

Yes, stay
my raven shaped sorrows,
once again
my shoulders shall be
your tree.

-*Heini Talip*-

Jump

At the edge of everything,
on the rim of my universe
is there a diving board
for us who want to jump?

And when you stand there,
does the divine darkness
purr or scream
at your impending splash?

-*Heini Talip*-

Raindrops

You know that sound
when you stand in the rain
and raindrops drum your umbrella?

I think that is the sound of my soul:

A human membrane being played
by the falling moisture of memories,
soaked
under never ending sorrow and silt
of simply being alive.

-Heini Talip-

Lost

I'm lost

and the travels of my tears
have no street signs.

Where to go

when darkness hangs on my lashes
and my cinnamon soul turns to a sandstorm.

-Heini Talip-

Place Called Soul

What is the name of the
bloom
littering my flesh
in my abyss

that place

with coughs of stardust,
where nights take refuge
from the flashlights

where my pain
leaves the luggage,
my nightmares
try on costumes

where the moths of the moon
pollinate my fears.

-Heini Talip-

Lonely Kind

My soul escapes
inside owls eyes,
to treetops
manicured with darkness,
into forests
of my lonely kind.

-Heini Talip-

Rise and Fall

Does the opening and closing
of my lids
ever rouse the grand orchestra?

Rise and fall.
    Rise and fall.
        Is that all?

-Heini Talip-

Lost Things

Beneath a thousand stars,
The jewel-toned tide turns,
The waves caress the sleeping shore,
Where a hairpin twinkles, lonely on the rocks,
Misplaced:

It shouldn't have been there.

No longer intact,
Like the girl it came with,
It glistens in the moonlight,
The sad stars twinkle back,
Sad because they can't unsee.

Lonely,
The silver and the sea

Wait — but she will not come looking,
Because she lost so much more than that.

-L. M. Steel

Crumbling

Silk-sleeve worn —and torn heart
unravelling,
Crumbling piece of ache:
Too many knives sliced through

Poor, poor throbbing thudding
Broken ramekin
of a heart,
There may never be enough glue.

-L. M. Steel

Chipped Nail Polish

I am just
Chipped nail polish,
Misophonia about to snap,
News Headline-fatigued,
Smudged eyeliner,
Injustice indignant,
Underpaid, sensitive old soul of
Secret madness,
Living in a time too loud!

-L. M. Steel

Hide There

In a thinner space than
Between a
Flittering firefly
And a fluttering butterfly
In a glittering summer sky,
I sit

In the fear
Of trying and flying,
And soaring
Or flailing and falling
And every outcome
In between:

And I hide there.

-L. M. Steel

No One Knows You

No one really knows you,
Your pendulum heart
Anxiously swinging from one throbbing thud to the next.
They see you, but *not really*,
You smile easily: muscle memory,
And when people ask how you do,
You tell them the good bits.
You talk a bit louder, to hear yourself over
the panic-pulse in your ears,
And they hear the high-pitched as joy,
They don't really hear you.
We give them what they came for:
A polite show,
Well-timed guffaws and anecdotal trades,

So they don't know —

that eloquent people don't know what to say,
that smiling people are not happy,
that people in love feel lonely,
that you are a vampire's prey:
haunted by apparitions of your first-day-at-school self
and the world still feels that way:
too big!

And every day is still
A bad swimming lesson,
You're keeping one foot on the floor:
No one looks below the water.
No one knows you, *not really*,
They cannot see beneath the surface,
You have covered it for too long with too many artefacts.
So, it's your fault,
Right?

-L. M. Steel

Woman in an Armchair

Sat here in a halo of dust and light,
You see me, illuminated, by a single sunray
seeping through the cracks of this blind,
I see you stop to see
A woman in an armchair.

With eyes I've come to read easier than rhyme,
I see you soak in the image,

You see: you think you see,
As you recognise beauty like it's an epiphany,
As a sun-drenched moment lifts complacency.

But you really only see
cheekbone,
brow, lashes:
Only a side profile too.
It is not the full picture.

And how I long to be seen.
To be peeled like a ripe nectarine,
To be opened up, petal by petal, like a Persian buttercup.
Time taken to see every single layer, line, corner, secret,
Close up

Beyond this portrait,
You cannot see I am hovering. I am not sat,
Tentative: on tenterhooks,
Unable to immerse in this armchair:
On call, for mother chores,
On edge, from haunting thoughts,
On lookout, in fixed fight or flight, of course.

You cannot see my heart,
A papier-mâché of love bruises,
You cannot see my battered ribs from anxious beating,
Nor can you see my weary bones beneath skin,
Faith beneath sin, wavering,
Lust and love savouring flesh

How I long to be seen completely,
Every layer all at once,
Not one moment at a time:
Colleague. Mother. Wife. Lover.

All of these things, blended, like the truth:
Intellectual and sensual, fragile and strong, sincere and pretending,
aching and healing, whole and broken, Woman

I yearn to be seen, truly,
Wholly,
In my flawed, unholy
Martyrdom.
Imperfect perfectionist,
longing for a break,
and an escape
and a thrill, all at the same time as
some peace.

But I think, even now,
I will always be seen
Piece by piece,
Most parts never visible to the human eye.

-L. M. Steel

What They Don't Say

It is not disease,
Just unease,
And in every way,
Except that you're
Not OK,
You must accept
You are OK.
That should ease you,
But not please you?
Must we plea with you
To please us
And free us
When there are pills
You could take
Anyway?
Any
way but this!

You don't need to
Go to sea
To see
Vast floating space,
You could just stay here,
And hear us
say nothing except,
there is nothing
anyone else could do-

And you could just pop the pills anyway

Pop to the Dr,
Pop the pills,
Pop back to us,
From that dark hole,
And everything else
Will pop back to perfect.

Easy.

-L. M. Steel

Welcome Back

A familiar hand on the small of my back,
A warm breath on my neck:
Secrets in my ear,
Whispering my inadequacies,
A hard knee pressed into my core beliefs,
Then the other hand around my neck.

How did he find me again?

No point fighting him off,
I slip out of my layers,
Lay down for him again,
Like always and
Let him enter:

Welcome back Anxiety.

-L. M. Steel

What Things Are Made Of

I sleep on a bed
I made
Of vows.
Next to a man
In a halo, I made
Of dreams.
Beside our babies
We made
Of love.
Within a bubble
Made
Of hope.

But...
Under the covers,
I am made of fear,
Behind this present
Is a past,
Made of ghosts.
In my soul I do not feel I was
Made good enough for any of this.

-L. M. Steel

Nightmares

Nightmares again, of the totalitarian state,
Where I crawl across shrapnel,
To the tune of cannons,
Aimed at those that defy the canon.

I am a heretic.

Recurring nightmares of
This chase, game of
Hide and seek where no one wins.
Power and control intertwined,
Neither of which are ever mine.

Maps banned,
Help withheld,
I am lost in this world
That is unreal, surreal, real.

When I wake up,
I will breathe
Relieved,
But I will never be free.

I will dream again -

But that is what becomes of those that live,
Terrorised within:
Not all wars are outside.

-L. M. Steel-

My Least Favourite

No, so much deeper than an urge:
I could ignore an urge.

More like a hankering — a yearn,
A malicious, unpalatable yearning
For you to know this feeling

Yes, how easily I forget
That of course I built you
The pedestal and you never asked for it
(And I really prefer it when
You're there where you belong,
You do too)

But then there are days
That you're so far away up there
That you can't see me
Wading, drowning

In a thick sludge of hateful misery —

It's true, misery likes company

And yet, here I am, alone.

So, stupidly, I sip the poison,
You know the one.

And in my dreams that scare me
I bite your face,
And I draw blood,
And I smother them,
And I walk as far away
As I can

So that when I am crying
It is reasonable for you to not hear me-

None of you.

In those dreams,
I give in to that hankering rage
And I drag the flesh of my most loved ones
Across glassy gravel
To see blood lined scrapes
On otherwise perfect skin

And I know I will hate myself
Even more when I wake up
And I will scrub my hands
As if it was real
When I scratched tissue from your bones
But there was no other way to make you cry too!

I know. I despair too, what a hateful girl?

It is not your fault that you can sleep through anything,
Is it?

It is no one else's fault
That at 3 in the morning
I am the only person
Awake in the world,
In the dark,
Tired in my stomach
Crying. Desperately sobbing
To a soundtrack
Of snoring
And faraway cars,
All going somewhere!

What sane or decent human could blame you for that?
I don't.

It is not blame:
It is bitterness,
Indignation,
Irritation,
Discontent,

It is ugly.
And no one loves a sad, angry girl
If she is ugly.

And so starts the lonely predicament (again)
Of pushing away,
And angry poems,
And angry dreams,
And pain seeking,
And pill popping,
Feeling blocking,
Downward spiral,
Into my least favourite
Familiar place.

-L. M. Steel

Panic Attack

The burn of cold sick,
The weight of old brick
On chest,
That tight, vice-like,
Strangled and tangled,
Frost-bite,
Heart-breaking
Plight
Of
Every pushed down scream and
Every flashback dream, that each
Unthreads another broken seam:
That's me.

But you wouldn't know.

-L. M. Steel

This Living

this living?
this is holy work.

this waking up each morning,
this routine, this cup of coffee,
this too-short shower & too-long commute.
this tossing & turning, this wondering,
this precious, all-too-human suffering.

this falling in & out of love with yourself,
with people who all look like connection
but taste wrong, this that feels like failure
but is a form of prayer.

with all your flaws,
you are still a holy being.
you carry within you seeds for new growth.
you reach out forever in all directions.

this living is moving inch by inch
toward something you can feel but cannot name.
this living is being terrified to change.

this living is finding out,
oh so slowly, that everything
you do & are is holy.

-Emily Adams-Aucoin-

Missing

I am lost
In my own home

The halls
Of my lonely
Heart

The echoing
Empty rooms
Of my soul

I wander
With a face
That isn't mine

Looking
For the corner
I may be
Hiding
In.

Lights are off
It is dark

I am groping
My way along
My own mind

Milk carton
images

Missing

Me.

-A. Brown-

Something Real

Can I find the right words
to explain every time
I sewed my mouth shut
and took that as a sign

it was better to be looked at
than heard or loved
because that's all I was worth
what they craved and I shrugged

off the pain that it brought
knowing that was the truth,
the reality of me
I looked in the mirror
and the only thing I could see

was a girl who could stab herself
in the heart just to feel
alive and to know
that something was real.

> I broke my own heart
> And bled myself silent
> But oh how they loved me
>
> In pieces...

-A. Brown-

Mess Of Myself

I walk around broken
Holding my own pieces together,
Gathering them up
As they fall away.

Armfuls of me,
Who I was,
Who I should be.
Trails of jagged edged expectations

Follow me everywhere I wander.

I cannot put myself back together.

Each hole an agonizing window
To the empty inside.
Sweep them up.

Where does each bit
Of constant disappointment fit?
Slide a fragment into place,
Band-Aid fix,
They are barely hanging on.
Fixated with cleaning up
This mess of myself.

- I have made a mess of myself.

-A. Brown-

Who Am I?

I have only ever known
how to live as a shadow
hide in plain sight
die and be reborn
wreck and rebuild
my own heart.

I have only every known
how to smile through pain
dance to bullet shots
beg to be seen
wish on burnt out stars
never meant for longing.

I have only ever known
how to paint content faces
sew tight skin
cobble feet two sizes too small
and wear each one as if

they belonged to me

I have only ever known
how to live in pieces
build boxes with lids for dreams
swallow the sound of my own voice
bury myself in the cold, black void.

Since I was young,
I have only ever known
This.

– how then can I answer
"who am I"?

-A. Brown-

Aching For Tomorrow

The night is silent
And suffocating.
A black abyss
Of endless thought.
I have reached the
End of my patience
For it.

Bring me the dawn.
The bright golden
Light of day.

Find me the sweet
Sonance of birds
and new beginnings.

Release my spent lungs.
This ever held
Long sharp breath.
I cannot bear
Another slow death

Of this old me.

The stone I shoulder
Awake and alone
In the dark
Is heavy and
I am aching
For tomorrow.

-A. Brown-

Chaos

The cluttered caverns
of chaotic minds
breed mystery and despair.
All the crazy more than thoughts
swirling everywhere.
The spirals of insanity
consuming the whole brain.
The thunderous roars
of second guessing
to drive someone insane.

-Abbey Forrest-

Disgraced

I stand disgraced.
Shame has ensanguined
my barely beating heart,
and now I'm devastated.
Nowhere to turn
All I can do is hide
And when I dig in deep
it's the demons I will have to fight.
No end in sight
as the life is choked from my very life,
I darken the doorways
and fold again inside.

-Abbey Forrest-

Choked

Steadily my own hands creep across my throat
choking the words out of my barren soul
A shell of who I used to be
Now forced by my own indignity
To silence the voice that would raise from the depths of me
All the while painting this fake life of tranquility
No one knows how much I died each day
Daring never to say the fears and torments
That dwelt within
My beastly flesh
Yet I digress
Because there are days when I feel so much less
Than the princess
I wish to be.

-Abbey Forrest-

The Overthinker's Battle

Some battle with the head
others with their heart
It's a little disturbing in my case
the two have joined forces
and riot against me daily.

-Abbey Forrest-

Inversion

In those less than
lucid moments
when logic inverts
into insanity
my veins burn with ice
as shards of glassy daggers
shred through my flesh.
The mind spins in spirals
descending into the
Abyss.

-Abbey Forrest-

Strangled

I've been Broken
Invisibly choked
While trying to evoke
Some compassion
From a passionless world
Force fed the words
I'm never quite enough
Consumed the deceit
Saying it's time
to give up
I'm strangled
gasp
Drop to the ground
Gagging on the lies
I devoured
I drown

-Abbey Forrest-

The Masking

This never ending circle
Of all the faces that I wear
Some are only borrowed
Yet no one seems to care
Let's not speak about it
We dare not say a word
"Sorry" is not a cure all
for behavior that is absurd.
Time has split between us
This tacenda we now own
Words we dare not let escape our mouths
while resentment builds its home.

-Abbey Forrest-

Lies

I'm fine.
It's all good.
You never ask questions
The way you should.
I'll be okay.
It's really true.
You only ask
For the sake of you.
Don't worry about it.
It ll work out.
Easier to say this
than tell you
you're the reason
I doubt.
It's okay
It's not your fault
my life is
crashing down.
Lies I tell you
As I lay on the ground.

-Abbey Forrest-

Leave Me Alone

Just leave me alone
Let me be
You see when you press
you show no respect for me.
I'll get there in my time
But you keep pushing the issue
But the issue is not yours...it's mine.
Let me deal with it in my own way
I know what's best for me
And right now you need to go away
You only press for your own selfish needs
Your concern really has nothing to do with me.

-Abbey Forrest-

Puppet Show

I feel like every day is a setup
I'm just a puppet in your show
Pull the string
Wind me up
Then you let me go.
And if by chance
I don't perform
you'll pull the string again
and lead me down the road
pretending you're my friend.
Again it happens and I fall
for your silly little line
That string you hold
you simply cut
and let me fall.
I die again inside.

-Abbey Forrest-

NightShade

There is this space
between love and hate
A line that must be drawn.
Where we lose the ability
To conversate
And all we feel is wrong.
It doesn't happen overnight
Little things are said
One is made to swallow down
All the lies they've been fed.
A drink of nightshade
To ease the pain
That's just where it starts
Taking in the poison
As it consumes your burdened heart
And when we stand upon that line
We're so easy to be swayed
Just a word is all it takes
For one to run away.

-Abbey Forrest-

Paradox of Promises

You are a
Paradox of promises
Too easily made
Yet never kept
Vowing inspiration
Leaving me in
Desperation
When all I sought was
clarification
You incinerated me with
malicious radiation
I will live to fight again.

-*Abbey Forrest*

Dissection

Under the microscope
Poked and prodded
Your thoughts not your own.
Dissected
Cut open for all to judge
Your life not your own.
Choked
Gagging on words
you are force fed
Your voice not your own.
So I plead with you
Come out from the judgement
that haunts you
Reclaim your life anew
Release the captivity of your mind
And let your voice shine through.

-*Abbey Forrest*

Veil of Silence

Enshrouded and cloaked
In a veil of silence
He never knows what to say.
Misjudged and abandoned
His words are scattered
And never come out the right way.
He moves with shadows
Only at night
Solitude is his friend
He speaks not a whisper
Too afraid to express
Even though she pleads with him.

-*Abbey Forrest*-

Dive

Holding my breath

I exist
in the hairline of my hollowness,
by the fringes of desolation,
dreaming of my demise.

Dive or
not today?

-*Heini Talip*-

Shopping

Happy pill
for the stinging ill,
there's never a bandage for the soul.

Try the apothecary balm,
maybe Amazon.com,
darkness on the sale rack tonight!

-Heini Talip-

Strings

If we are strings,
are we knotted at the ends?
Do they form hearts,
joints, our folds at the bends?
If we are strings,
what melodies do we play?
Are we attached to clouds,
gray, lonely, and stray?
If we are strings,
what happens when we break?
Do we fall deeper,
or do we wake?

-Heini Talip-

Little Bush Fires

You gas-lighted
behind closed doors,
Little bush fires everywhere
that nobody saw,
I held the truth
between gritted teeth,
As if your secrets
were mine to keep,
Could not cut you out,
So cut me instead,
Healing the ache,
As teenage wrists bled.
Found an extinguisher-
Opened my mouth,
Let go of your grip,
And the truth spilled out
Into a forest fire,
For everyone to see,
Blades set down:
I was free.

-L. M. Steel

Hive

A hive of self-doubt buzzes:
And again I sit in its hum
To meditate on this song
Every day anew,
The vibrations reverberate in my soul,
Why can't I just lay in a lavender field instead of
In the endless burn of uncertainty

-L. M. Steel

Sonder

Again, harassed:
A chaotic mess,
Consumed by lists,
The chores and stress

Short fuse, guilty,
Self-absorbed really,
Can think of nothing but all this,
Well, nearly:

Then I see you,
And I'm full of sonder,
You're cold, hungry
And I can't help but ponder,

Did you once stress about lists and chores?
Before you slept outside shop doors,
What would you do now to have such stress?
Instead of sleeping in strangers' mess,

For a single moment when you catch my eye,
I think I know you but that's not right,
It's just that we both think the same,
It could be me there, I can't complain.

-L. M. Steel

Day 1 at Home

We're making cards for the baby,
It's picture perfect.
Glue and crayons, everything becoming stuck together.
So stuck.
A glittery trail: a happy mess.
But all that glitters
is not gold.
I praise the choice of colours
Half-heartedly
Distracted, I methodically plan
How the hell I will tidy this all up.

Clock-watching,
Breath-counting,
Spinning and somersaulting
Across a spectrum of emotion
From one angry end
To the *never-ending* blessed other.

Daddy would put a hand
On my arm right now,
And I'd breathe out better.
But he's back in the world of the living today.
Hot coffee and thank-yous.

Task-finishing,
Phone-checking,
Tired but efficient, ticking off lists
Across a day broken up by breaks
and tea and adult conversation,
From one tired start
To its satisfying end

-L. M. Steel

Bold Hearts

Why do we always question
Our bold hearts:
And not know we are strong?
We plunge into self-doubt
Every night
To swim the colossal length and breadth

Of it —
And back again.
Every morning we awake, to
Look hopelessly into the mirror:
Our own face a haze
As Anxiety stares back,
With his merciless eyes,
When will we learn to ignore
Such harsh reflections,
And embrace self-compassion instead?

-L. M. Steel

Worry Cycle

Kaleidoscope kid:
Kid that brings such delight and worry,
Worry, I do every night, that I can't protect you.
You from the heart-thief wolves,
Wolves in sheep's clothing that will walk you home,
Home, where I worry will not always be the safety it is now,

Now, while you are small enough to sleep in my arms.

Darling, I worry because I know what the world becomes,

Becomes a black hole or a shadow valley,
Valley of man-ghosts, where cat-calls seep into dreams,
Dreams become nightmares and flashbacks rolling,
Rolling you over into fear.

Sweet child of my heart, I burst,
Burst with love that cannot stretch its protective arms far enough,
Enough to reach across the years,

Years that are slipping away too quickly

Quickly my love becomes panic,
Panic that the world won't change in time,
Time will turn you into a woman and this -

This is not a woman's world.

-L. M. Steel

Growing Pains

Constellation of sad sighs,
Fallen stars in faraway skies,
Lava love bubbling over lyrical lies,
Pounding heart under prying eyes,

Pathflower appearing through drought demise.
Pain: the fertile soils for growing wise

-L. M. Steel

Jump

If you stood on the edge of the world -
would you jump?
I've stood on one leg,
a foot dangling off the side
just to feel something
other than fear.
Adrenaline clogs my ears -
silence deafening.
Sometimes my mind
is too loud for my body.
A stranger stands on
the edge beside me -
smoking cigarettes and cheating death.
I wonder if we held hands
if our arms could look like
a human paper chain
blowing in the wind,
a decoration to celebrate
the opposite of loneliness...

-Eloise

Candy Dots

I line up my antidepressants
in the morning like those
colored dot candies
you rip off the sheet of paper
with your teeth –
pink and yellow and blue
coating my tongue with
promises for a better tomorrow
when my mind has already
convinced me that tomorrow
will not be good
or better
or best.
I swallow the pills
with coffee as my chaser,
a silent prayer that the
best day is yet to come...

-Eloise-

Happiness Lives Next Door

All is not lost just because
you haven't found where
your happiness lives yet.
I have knocked on all the neighbors' doors
with chocolate chip cookies - hopeful -
peering in through the windows
to see a glimpse of how the other half lives,
joy hung up in the mudroom
next to a child's raincoat.

-Eloise-

Forgiveness

If my soul could speak -
Would she forgive me?
I have found Depression
in her corner for all these years,
and let them be neighbors,
but she's never called the cops.
I am waiting for the day
that Harmony comes out to play,
if only for a moment...

-Eloise-

Hope in a Hurricane

I can't make eye contact
with the person in the mirror
who asks me to love her.
I grab places of my body
that feel heavy in my hands
and smudge the glass
with my fingertips
to erase the mistakes.
She begs me to find
one beautiful thing
among the wreckage -
hope in a hurricane...

-Eloise-

Grow

We are all just wilted flowers in the end,
hoping someone will take
a watering can to our flaws -
and watch us grow anyway.

-*Eloise*-

Elixir to Life

The challenge today is joy.
Sometimes I wonder if going on a run would cure me,
if my sweat could glisten instead of weigh down my skin,
if forcing a smile in the mirror could erase the worry wrinkles,
if going out in the sun could fix the dark.
Maybe the elixir to life - to today -
is the fact that lipstick on a coffee cup can be poetry, too.

-*Eloise*-

Untitled 43

Water is only beautiful
if you can swim.
Can't you see that I have drowned before?
My hair is still wet.

- *Maya Elphick*-

Giving Up On Me

Giving up on me
to join those all-seeing giants,
set with jewels that shine above the clouds
and house the lonely souls in nightgowns.
Giving up on me
and all my sunny misadventures
and the semi-precious daydreams
I lay amongst poetry.
Giving up on me
chewed nails and all, ink stained locks of hair
and just one page to spare,
I will not share, I will not share.
Giving up on me
because I refuse to give up
and all the skin and bone and broken phones
and jeans that rip and feet that trip.
Giving up on me
giving up on
giving up
giving
give in.

- Maya Elphick-

The Artist

My cup fills
with the tears shed
for the girl who throttles bottle necks.
Grip so tight she can barely breathe,
barely see beneath a smile that's just teeth.

She stares into the eyes
of her green glass reflection,
stranger's complexion.
Crushing cans beneath her feet
in the hope her soles might bleed.

The canvas on her wrist
begs to be kissed and healed by kind lips.
Scars traced by fingertips,
serrated bottle tops
and rusty razors:
all the things she keeps
in pillowcases.

The red stains on the carpet
aren't always merlot
and the sips aren't slow
and she slips on snow,
sugar around her nose,
anything to silence the low voices
she can't control.

And now I'm crawling across
these glass shards
reaching out towards the girl,
splayed like art
on bathroom tiles,
fragile heart
in birthday smiles.
Her voice is so small,
I'll put mine in her pocket.
I'll grow her tall,
I'll fix her up,
I'll heal the girl
and make her art once more.

- Maya Elphick -

Dawn

The night dies
like all other things
that beat.

Watch the sun rise,
I have been waiting
for you to meet.

- Maya Elphick -

The Morning Comes Slow

The morning comes slow.
Crawling up the dark
night sky like
aching fingertips
of burning bright light,
eager to tighten
their grip on the world.

My heart races in time
with each ray,
pounding in my
chest like the drums
of an ancient vessel

pushing me on through
my own murky thoughts,
my mind a violent taskmaster.

How often have I held on
In the darkness as my seas
are ravaged by storms of
my own making?
My hands weak from
Holding on to myself,
I beg for the calm
that comes at the
end of the long voyage
through the fear
and the black.

Gradually my eyes
are filled with the
welcomed golden dawn
and the drums quiet
their incessant throbbing
song in the deep.

I find I have survived
the swells once again
and come home safely
out of the anxious
jaws of swallowing midnight.
It is a new day and I rise
triumphant with the sun.

- I dread each looming twilight

-A. Brown-

Always, Always

I close my eyes
In the darkness
Of yet another
Long
Agonizing night
And promise myself

That despite it all...

My lungs will fill with air
My eyes will open to the sun
My legs will carry me from this bed

And
I will try again
Tomorrow.

-there will always, always be tomorrow...

-A. Brown-

I Am Not

Each morning
I rise from this bed,
stand on these
two strong legs
and gently undress
my self loathing.

Slowly

It slips to floor
as I unbutton its grasp,
step out of the heavy
weight.
I pull over my head
it's thin, clingy need.

Exposed.

My self hate
is wrinkled
from wrestling with it
in the night,
torn in the fight
for myself.
It is soiled
and stained
with my own tears.

Ruined.

But I
Am not.

I am not.

-A. Brown-

Refuge

I often go there...my refuge.
There where the wind mercilessly
whips my hair around and into my
face, stinging my eyes as I walk
along the dusky ocean shoreline.

Warm, frothy water pools
around my bare ankles,
obscuring my feet from view.

Isn't this just like life?

Hurting in the most beautiful
of places.

Hiding parts of us in the
dark unknown.

And yet, we come back...
We always come back...

-A. Brown-

<u>Me</u>

I feel it,
Bone deep...

She is shaking.
She is breaking.
Free.

I feel it,
in my soul...

She is quaking.
She is aching.
See.

I feel it
burning fire...

She is waking.
She is make
and unmaking.

She is
Me.

-A. Brown-

<u>Stars On My Eyelids</u>

I draw stars on the backs of my eyelids at night.
My mind traces the shape from tip to tip
Each point an anchor to my reality.

Breath in...

Breath out...
Habitual evening sketching ritual.
Over and over until the darkness in my thoughts
Resembles the heavens above my existence,

Pulling me up and out of my own disquiet.
One by one they light the inky black
of angst filled introspection.

Self made constellations leading me to the center of myself.
Grounded in the compulsion of consistent
Repetitious depictions.

Outlines of luminary celestial edges lulling me
Out of the roaring in my cognizance
And finally, into the quiet cradle of dormancy.
At night, I draw stars on the backs of my eyelids.
My mind traces the shape from tip to tip
Each point and anchor to reality

Breath in...

Breath out...

-A. Brown-

We Can Save Ourselves

Deep in the dark
and destructive nature
of my own wounded soul
lies a small pin hole of light.
Pricked and forced open
by the long thin line
of generations
of effeminate voices
whispering the bones
of their backs
and the weight
of their voices,
razor sharp,
into this stone heavy
masochistic heart.

Mother to mother to mother
back
to the beginnings of time.
Each in their turn
reaching through
the microscopic

breach in me,
created by their own will
carried in their blood to mine:
ripping wide the stone encasement
in which
my self annihilating tendencies lie.
The luminous resulting blaze
of autogenous realization
blinding In its
astonishing revelation.

Who can tell me
I cannot stand?

Who can tell me
I cannot heal?

Who can tell me
I cannot live?

-Not even I.
For their strength
Is my strength.

Their voices
my voice.

And we can save ourselves.

-A. Brown-

The Art of Precious Scars

We cried together, you and I
Deep in those dark nights
Of our first early years
Both longing for something
We couldn't give ourselves
Needing to be soothed
But finding no succor

And remember those long days
Where even the sunshine on my arms
Felt wrong?
I sat by the window, staring out
Holding you and counting
Each car as it passed by
Through teary eyes.
It kept my mind from wandering
To darker thoughts.

We took long drives
Because you wouldn't sleep
And I couldn't.
You felt the rumble of the road
Under your tiny body
Lull you into a half daze.
I fully felt the pain of being broken
Somewhere in my mind.
The radio sounded so distant,
Background noise to the music
Of my own anguished sobs.

Maybe you recall the afternoons
Spent crawling in your shut room
Roaming from toy to toy
Happily playing as I lay there on the floor
Staring at the wall, willing it
To open up and swallow me whole.

You would smile at me and I would
Reach out, as if you could keep me
From falling over the edge.
Someone else could do this right for you,
I thought. Someone else who isn't me.

We held each other too, though.
When it was just the two of us
Drifting off to sleep.
Your hand wrapped around my finger.
My heart wrapped around your existence.
A piece of my soul on the outside.
It can't all be just jagged pieces,
If this moment feels whole.

You and me, we were Kinstsugi
Gold melded into the cracks.

-A. Brown-

And So Will I

There is a burning
in my chest that
lights the way
forward out of
the long dark night.

A small persistent voice

that speaks to me
in the deep of

my need telling me
this is not the end.

Heart beats drumming
a steady line of hope,
a persuasive song
of a new and
everlasting tomorrow
that will not die.

The sun will rise
with a steadfast
flaming fire.

And so will I.

-A. Brown-

Heavy

we are carrying the weight.
some,   more than others.
but all of us Atlas,
collectively.

& what would happen if we
set it down?
but this is not something that
can be done gracefully.

this is a final untying.

most, when untethered, float
somewhere that
may be Heaven, or Hell,
but we don't know. so we hold on.

attempt to create a peace
that lasts under this gravity.

attempt to re-calibrate all of
this heavy.

attempt to shoulder it all more
efficiently.

-Emily Adams-Aucoin-

A Dream

in a dream,
you carved
a lover from
soft, red clay
with your
softer, trembling
hands.

in a dream,
you carved a
kind face &
a body that
could only touch
yours with love.

in a dream,
you carved your
own eyes
& mouth
& hands
into blessed clay.

& in a dream,
that was enough.

-Emily Adams-Aucoin-

Love as Sugar

I am in awe
of the beauty
we create
from suffering.

we take the
lemons that life
gives us

& bless them,
hand them
tenderly to our
children,

teach them to
squeeze out the
sour & most
importantly:

how to sweeten.

-Emily Adams-Aucoin-

Despite

I want to start by saying
I am grateful,
That this living is
enough, enough, enough

but when no one is watching.
I have been known to hold
my hands open to the sky
in wanting.

when the emptiness becomes
too much.

I watch the birds flutter,
making a home in a space
above our doorway

& they seem happy,
perfectly happy,

despite the smell from the
sewage plant across the street,

despite the cracked & crumbling
structures, the decaying foundation.

& then why should I not be
able to do the same?

& what exactly, is missing?

I know it is important,
Anyway. I know it cannot be named.

-Emily Adams-Aucoin-

Wildflowers

there are wildflowers growing
in the front yard
(if you could
call it that) of this crumbling
apartment complex.

but this is not that type of
poem.

the type where I see
them as more than flowers,
as a sign for something
better coming.

I do not
water them tenderly, do
not notice their small & unlikely
growth.

I do not
hinge my happiness, my hope,
on something so insignificant,
so fleeting, &

certainly, I do not
need to say that I do not
cry when I see them one
day, shriveled
beneath
construction equipment.

I do not find meaning in this,
of course.
I do not find meaning in this.

-Emily Adams-Aucoin-

Coming Storm

lately, I have been more
coming storm than person.

& this is not
a metaphor for my depression.

there is a cleansing coming,
I know it. I can feel my skin
tightening,

suddenly too small & flimsy
to carry all of this love,
this heavy empathy.

so if I cry,
it's because
the grasses look   thirsty.

& if I scream, it's in release.

& if there's damage, I swear
it will have been done
accidentally.
           collaterally.

to atone, I will make all my words
drip apology. but still, I have learned
that some storms are necessary.

-Emily Adams-Aucoin-

It Comes & Goes

I sat at the edge of the world,
feet dangling in some
foreign ocean,
darkness dancing behind
my eyes, wondering
if healing also
comes in
waves.

-Emily Adams-Aucoin-

Endless

there is so much space between
who I am
& who I want to be
that it
gives me vertigo.

but in the morning light,
I am endless.

I stretch from here
until sundown.

& I could do anything,
anything.

I could be anything.

-Emily Adams-Aucoin-

Lightly

sometimes, this life
is less soft grass path
& more

kaleidoscope of
fish hooks
& well-disguised
traps with teeth.

which is to say:
in order to survive,
you must learn

when to step lightly.

-Emily Adams-Aucoin-

Still

I am trying to care
less about how this
body looks &
more about the
way it works.

I bless each
shaking breath.
every clumsy step.

still, my thoughts
grow blades.

-Emily Adams-Aucoin-

Storm

it is too early
to tell whether
I have been

weakened or
strengthened

by this storm.
but I think the
worst of it

is over, &I am
still
holding
on.

-Emily Adams-Aucoin-

A Quiet Mind, a Roaring Heart

most of those thoughts i've worked out by now
mind races until i let them drown out
a few deep breaths usually does the trick
a sweet self-reminder "I am enough"
also helps me with the ridding of it
the thoughts I can handle
the dreams though
the dreams are another beast
and they take no prisoners

-M.R.S.-

Always More

if all we do is chase perfection
and constant self-improvement
will we not realize the beauty
in what we already are
will we trap ourselves in empty jars
and label them "never enough"

-M.R.S.-

Stigma

It is not disgraceful.
But it is not graceful
Either:

It does not glide,
Or pirouette,
From some Swan Lake dance:
It is not a swan.
It is just the furious paddle beneath water that no one sees.

It is not a star,
Or the glisten of a star,
But the falling star that no one wished on.
A lost star. A hole in the sky.

It is not a floral bouquet:
It is not a rose.
It is the secret hiding within a bud.
It is not a gift, it is contraband.
It is not a beautiful thing.

But -
It doesn't have to be ugly either,
Or such a dirty secret,
Not really.

We could just lift this veil,
Expose the struggle,
Put the truth out there,
Ungracious, yes
But it's not disgrace.

-L. M. Steel

These Lines

Frown lines–
From a heavy heart and a mind pensive,
From fragility, empathy and worries extensive.

Hurt lines–
From anger, fear, angst, despair,
Surviving teenage life was hard to bear,

Stretch lines–
From growing, carrying, bringing to earth,
From making lives that gave me worth

Fault lines–
The tectonic plates of my temper,
The heat of which I can't attemper

Between these lines–
Where insecurities sow,
Against all odds, wildflowers grow.
From the pain and anguish I've come to know,
These flaws let wisdom and kindness flow.

-L. M. Steel

Gardening

Pruning this overgrown garden,
Tending to these tangled stems, again,
Ripping weeds from roots,
Pulling out uninvited shoots,
Repotting reluctant seeds.

Thorns in fingers,
Soil under nails,
Nettles biting at ankles,
Wasps watching for crumb-lined skin to scavenge,

Bitten, stung, scarred,
To make everything right —

For the sun and the rain
To laugh at me,
Make it all grow again
By next summer

Out the tools will come,
Determined sweat-soaked muscles will ache,
To beat nature

This is therapy, I think:
I will put in all this work again
But I cannot change nature

I will always be an overgrown garden
Of wildflowers and tangled branches,
It might be time to just enjoy its beauty.

-L. M. Steel

Table For One

Please be kind to the gentle hearts
who dine by themselves
and toast to love.

- Maya Elphick-

She Ran With Me

She ran with me even when
the shoes made our heels bleed.
The land was crimson
by the end of our journey
but we had rosy cheeks.

- *Maya Elphick*

24K

Rise above the
stiff collars
upstanding on rough necks.
Middle-aged men
with sawdust skin
and tight lipped grins.

Look down upon
those gold plated
play dates and
red-rimmed wine glasses,
washed sheets
and shameful deeds in the dark.

Walk straight past
those stilettos
and the candy man
and every Goddamn thing
they wave beneath your nose
that carries a price tag.

Don't let the bastards get you down, honey.
You'll never need them like they need you.

- *Maya Elphick*

The Writer

Do not be afraid to
wreck with your words
or punch in your pages
when the world needs a fighter
and all you have is a pen.

- *Maya Elphick-*

Just try...

Try to tear me down
I dare you
Try to shake my faith
It ll scare you
The strength i have inside
I have no fear
because i stand I the light
You ll fail every time
because I been through it all
Lies and deceit
My resilience is power
You ll never defeat
I ll never cower
Just you wait and see
I stand unshaken because
There's a warrior in me.

-*Abbey Forrest-*

Deceit

Broken promises
Hidden lies
Falling each
And every time
When is it enough
To stop the fall
To just stand up
And say fuck it all.

-Abbey Forrest-

Continuing

I've been pouring out
all I have
and will continue to drain
endlessly
shining my light
I won't hold back
or refrain
no matter what
I will press on
And stand firm
In my beliefs
I will not bend or break
Or bow my knee to
Those faithless thieves.

-Abbey Forrest-

Protected Heart

The promises from a poisoned mind
Will twist and tangle you
The power of an untruthful being
Will grab and wring you through
Let not the roots of evil things
penetrate your soul
Guard your joy
protect your heart
and be just who you are.

-Abbey Forrest-

The Hidden

In the shadows to the side
Under covers where I hide
No one seeking
Never found
Still I wonder
Should I make a sound
If I speak will they turn
Will they mock or will I
burn
Never knowing what to say
Never trusting my own way
Turning inward
Then I'll find
Peace within in me
Strength divine
Learning to be
Just who I am
Discovering I'm good
enough
Where I stand.

-Abbey Forrest-

Scarred Strength

It's in the tattered pages
of our stories
where innocence
is surrendered.
We paste, glue and tape
The rips within our book.
The perfect papers,
forever fractured,
regardless of the healing.
The tearstained pages,
forever scarred,
however, show our strength.
It's in these wounds
that hope and joy emerge
and strengthen us in faith.

-Abbey Forrest-

Cut Deep

I carried your words
on my shoulders for
far too long.
Dragged them
behind me for years
like a beaten dead horse.
The weight of them
cut deep lines into my mind.
They began to rot
inside my heart.

I picked myself apart
over your mistreatment
of my gentle love until
I was left with gaping
wounds along my thin skin.
Pieces of flesh falling
In piles all around my
room as I paced wide ruts
into the floorboards,
contemplating the reasons
why your soft mouth hid sharp
objects in its warm exhalations.

The night I stretched
myself bloody on a rack to
reach your high expectations
was the same night you cut me
in half, brought me low in two
for your own amusement.
I searched for the missing bits
of me in the dark,
and realized you were
already walking away
with the most precious
ones, whispering your
malignant indifference
to my pain
on the way out.

I gathered my guts,
sewed myself together,
swept up my old remains,
laid new planks
and boxed up my
masochistic tendencies.
I cut loose the necrotic
burden of your
cadaverous influence
on my laden soul
and left it to crawl
your words
back to you.

*-now my words carry you
in their truth.
I hope they cut deep.*

-A. Brown-

Self Liberation Howlings

I don't write
What you want
To hear.

I write my truth.
The dark

Parts of me,
Pulled up
From the
Silent places
I hide in.
Uncomfortable
Relatability
Is my song.
A mirror to
What may also
Be hiding in
You.
Have you
Let it out yet?

My words
Are life.
My own.
A full belly's
Worth of substance.
Bite them off
And chew.
Walk away full
Of the whole

Of me,
Empty of the
Habitual norm.

These letters
Strung into
Sentences
Hold my
Secrets
And speak
My fears.
Life boat,
Resuscitation:
They bring

Me back
From the dead.

I write to save.
I write to redeem.
I write myself
Alive again.

-A. Brown-

Scars

You couldn't tell
It starts out small

Each act you take
That builds a wall
Around your heart
That keeps you from
Yourself,, the truth
What you've become.

It's fine You say
And go along
Thinking this is what
will make you strong
With each brick a letting go
Of self and dreams
Of all you know

Until one day

You're safe behind
The very thing
You now must climb

To free yourself
From doubt and pain
A strangers face
An unknown shame

And piece by piece
You break on through
To the place where you
remember you
And realize it
was all a lie
You didn't need
An alibi
You are perfect now
Just as you are
You don't need
To hide your scars

-break down your walls
let the light shine on who you are.
-A. Brown-

Liberated Creature

This caged bird,
broken wings
no longer sings...
has found a way
to fly.

I write the wind
under my chest
pen the rest...
the sun, the moon
the sky.

These words
they lift me
wild and free...
My song, my voice
my cry.

- liberated creature

-A. Brown-

Lost In The Wild Of Me

Build yourself a ladder,
made from the pieces
of bone and soul
I've carved from myself
day in and day out
as I whittle away
my own truth.

Scale these high walls,
made from bricks
of lies and wishes

I've skillfully molded
into the shape
of a stranger
to hide the strange

shape of me.

Peer into my mind,
made from good intentions
and crippling fear
I've fashioned into
functioning chaos
so I can walk
through my life
without a spine.

Reach in and pull me up,
the one made from
light and beauty
I've hidden somewhere
deep down along
the soft edges
of a sharp and
wild heart.

-don't fall in.
-don't get lost

in the wild of me.

-A. Brown-

After All This Time

For years now you have traced the lines of
every rolling curve with knowing fingers.
Followed the well worn paths that time
and gravity have etched into the outer layers
of who I am. Though the landscape changes
with each turn of season, your steady gait still
echoes through. A careful course you've charted,
each step a welcomed familiar sound in the deep

of the wood.

Your eyes have swallowed in every inch of body
and breath. The rise and fall of chest as
celebrated as the rise and fall of the sun along
the vast horizon. Each turn and bend like a
flowing river memorized, reverenced for its
natural power and simple rippling beauty. Here
you have so often lain quietly along my shore.
Here you have rested your weary head in the

comfort of the grass.

How well then, do you know the darkness that
gathers in the corners of the mind? Have you run
your hand along the jagged edges of thought
that protrude from the soft places I try to hide
in? Cut yourself and bled wondering among the
thorny wilderness of my wild heart? How often
have you roamed through the miles of wreckage
and debris left behind from a lifetime of
breaking?

Have you...
That is to say...

    After all this time,

        Do you really know me at all?

-A. Brown-

Despite Me

Thank you for loving me,
            despite me.

        That's no small feat.

            (even I cant do that sometimes)

-A. Brown-

Changed

Of the few
things in this world
that have thankfully
remained

constant

what a surprise it is
to discover
that am thankfully
a thing that has

changed.

(consistently)

-A. Brown-

Dolls and Dragons

I used to be proud of my beauty.
Wore it like a badge.
"Who will tell me what I'm worth today?" I wondered
as men cat called and whistled,
looked me up and down and measured
while I winked and laughed,
empty inside.
I pulled up my hair and painted on my face.
Perfection covered pain because scars aren't pretty
and pretty is important if you want to be somebody.
Nobody wants a body that curves and moves
like mountains.
Only one that stays still and stands straight
like hard plastic with a thin frame, white toothed smile,
Long light hair.
I can be that.
So I was.

That, and that and that...
"what do you want?" id ask them all
as I shed my skin.
New mask, prettier shell, hollow
a doll.
But now I'm older, and wiser, and wider and softer.
I'm deeper and darker haired,
with gnashing teeth and magnificent wings.
I roar and breath fire when they call out,
quaking the ground as I step by.
Burning inside.
Because I know I am real and full of power
and scars are truth and I am worth lifetimes
of my own love.
Fierce with thick skin, thicker thighs, my own face, broken shell
filled up with more than a fading badge of beauty.
A dragon.

-A. Brown-

Surprise

you would be surprised, I think,
at how much it takes to break a person,

to crush that little,
preserving & durable thing
inside them that makes them love the world
even when it stings,

even when it
burns & curls them up at the edges.

you would be surprised how much the world
can hurt & keep turning anyway,

how it can take & take & take
but then, without warning
or deserving, give.

you would be surprised at how
every morning,
the thrushes sing to the new day,

& how they sound not even a little surprised
but sure, & thankful.

-*Emily Adams-Aucoin*-

A Good Day

today is a good day.

today, I do not feel
my inevitable
mortality,

do not hear the
ticking, the
counting down.

I do not see
bodies of the
once-living
lining the road on
my way to work,

& when I touch my
skin, I feel my body
humming,
my heart
thumping,

everything so
alivealivealive.

-Emily Adams-Aucoin-

The Art of Not Wanting

I go to the desert alone, with
what little I have, to sit in the sand
& burn away what is left.
I am here to learn the art of *not wanting*,
the stripping this life
to the bone
& knowing beauty bare.

I unfold clumsily,
a flower with too many
heavy petals, & try to listen.

to understand the lesson.

hours later, when the sun bows
beneath the horizon, I walk back to
my car.

I come away with nothing.
I come away with everything.

-Emily Adams-Aucoin-

After You

I used to dress this
heart in darkness,
in apathy–

a necessary sacrifice
for all the
small funerals.

now, in each
moment, there is
something
new
to call beautiful.

-Emily Adams-Aucoin

Stretch Marks

I notice a dozen
small
& unfamiliar
stretch marks
on my hips,

& think back
to the years
I counted the
calories in
toothpaste

& saw bone as
beautiful.

& so to my new
stretch marks,
I say:
welcome.

-Emily Adams-Aucoin

Small Talk

when I say: hello,

I mean: look at the way
                 the sun refuses to
                 abandon you no
                 matter what dark
                 thing you may do.
&
when I say: how are you?

I mean: I can see your eyes
                 have sunken,
                 darkened,
                 glazed.
&
when I say: have a good day,

I mean: I know the night
                 has been long. the
                 light is coming.
                 hold on.

-Emily Adams-Aucoin-

The Gift

teach me how to wrap
this world so that
they,
fledglings wide-eyed
& not wholly willing,
will open it.
will see it as gift.
too much
sorrow for paper,
& too heavy to carry.

but look, how beautiful.
how forgiving,
how
necessary.

-Emily Adams-Aucoin-

Love Letter

this world & I are
hopelessly in love.

never eye-to-eye
but always trying,

we speak in *staying*,
in hands-grasping-soil

thank you for this
bounty.

(I won't leave until
it's time.

not until
it's time.)

-Emily Adams-Aucoin-

A Goal, Four Ways

I have one simple
yet lofty goal:

to love the world
as it is.

to bathe in all its
beauty.

to live as well &
as lightly as I can.

to praise until the
very end.

-Emily Adams-Aucoin-

Coincidentally

she got lost searching for reason
until she tucked her yearning for meaning
in her back pocket
and let her existence lead the way

-M. R. S.-

Paradox

that's when the path turned dark
the willow trees loomed
something grew from the ground
mold i think
i saw an old, rickety bridge in the distance
i knew it wouldn't hold my weight
no life in sight
but a crow
it gave me a cunning stare
i somehow still trusted it
it got darker
as i hesitated toward the bridge
i walked by an old bench
someone else had sat here
a message in a bottle
i unscrewed the cap
opened the message
it said nothing
no help from the presence I thought once there
i looked toward that old bridge
it swayed in the wind
an epiphany overwhelmed me
the problem with believing
everything happens for a reason
is that you have to trust the path you're on
no matter how dark
no matter how uncertain

M.R.S.-

The Journey Home

at long last i had arrived
alone but not lonely
a great triumph indeed
i relished in solitude
finally comfortable as me
it took a long while though
as any voyager knows
to adjust my sails
breathe in, and just be

M.R.S.-

You're Okay

look at the universe
know you are okay
thank the universe
for allowing you to be okay
thank god for giving you to the universe
and the universe to you
breathe in earth's air
notice how it saves you
every moment you breathe it in
you are okay
you are saved
life is good

M.R.S.-

Emily Aucoin-Adams

Emily Adams-Aucoin grew up in Upstate New York, but now lives, works, and writes in inner-city Baton Rouge, Louisiana with her loving husband, Brent. Emily works as a middle school English Language Arts teacher, where she exposes as much poetry to her students as the curriculum allows (and sometimes more). She has been writing poetry since the age of twelve and is inspired by nature, the human condition, and how both interact and cannot exist without the other. She often writes of her struggle with anxiety, depression, and disordered eating to raise awareness and show others that they are not alone in their suffering. Her poetry has been published in various literary magazines (After the Pause, K'in, Cagibi), and she posts original poetry on her Instagram page @emilyapoetry.

Ashleigh Brown

Ashleigh Brown, more commonly known among her followers as simply A. Brown, is a full-time wife and mother who spends her free time conjuring up poems. Writing has always been a passion of hers, but she discovered poetry's power to express thoughts and feelings in creative and constructive avenues during the tumultuous years of high school. Today she still uses poetry as a means of self-expression and cathartic healing. Brown tends to write about the experiences that inspire her: anxiety, depression, self-empowerment, and even her past. Her passion for writing can be seen in her use of long-form poems that capitalize on brilliant usages of imagery and rhyme to draw out emotions and drive home truths. Her poetic roots are founded in such greats as Mary Oliver, William Stanford, and Charles Bukowski.

Eloise

Photo Credit: Emma Frances Logan

Eloise is a 20-something with a typewriter collection and coffee running through her veins. She is constantly searching for the right words to describe the tiny, beautiful moments scattered across our everyday lives. When not scouring the shelves of used bookstores in Charlotte, North Carolina, she's dabbling in the written word on Instagram at eloise_the_typewriter. She always carries an open book and an open heart.

"Take a poet and gift her your presence,
and she will give you her heart disguised as prose,

spilled ink tears, and words eternal..."

-Eloise

Maya Grace Elphick

Maya Elphick is a student of Arts living in rural Norfolk, UK, with her various pets including three dogs and a bearded dragon. Her interests include film, photography, music, wildlife and literature. Her passion for poetry developed in 2014 after discovering the works of poets such as Charles Bukowski and Maya Angelou (her namesake). Writing soon became an important part of her life as she found poetry to be a natural and therapeutic way of expressing and understanding her feelings, , while creating something that endures even when the feeling does not.

Abbey Forrest

Abbey Forrest is the author of the Stirred Moments poetry series. She is also currently working on a children's series of poetry books. Born in the Pacific Northwest, she spent much of her childhood hiking and playing in the woods giving her a pure and organic love and appreciation for trees, mountains and other amazing creations in nature. She draws inspiration from such authors as CS Lewis, Henry David Thoreau and Ralph Waldo Emerson, Abbey Forrest holds similar ideals to be true: that life is sweet and very short; take nothing for granted; make the most out of every moment you're given. Having grown up in the Pacific Northwest, she has a pure and organic love and appreciation for trees, mountains and other amazing creations in nature.

M.R.S.

Hailing from Inver Grove Heights, MN, Morgan Short is a 25 year old emerging poet and writer, signing her works with her initials M.R.S. With a degree in Journalism - Strategic Communications from the University of Wisconsin-Madison, Morgan has always been interested in telling stories, whether it be through journalism, marketing, short stories or poetry. Lifting a pen means inviting others into her world and exploring ways she can step into the worlds of others. Born with a condition called hemihypertrophy, much of her writing is inspired by her struggle with body image. Morgan's guiding forces in her life are her parents, Jodi and Will and her younger siblings, Jake and Taylor.

L. M. Steel

Born in 1986, L.M. Steel was born in West London and has had a passion for writing from a young age. Since graduating from Kent University, she has built a career working with young disadvantaged people. Steel has since returned to writing poetry, using it to highlight issues such as mental health, sexual assault and motherhood. Steel lives with her husband and two children.

Heini Talip

An avid writer since childhood, scribbling stories on folded papers, diaries, and notebooks, Heini Talip has always found solace in words. An aspiring poet, she often embraces the melancholic and dark tones in herself. Born and raised in Helsinki, Finland, she moved to South Texas after a pen-pal relationship turned to love. Writing both about the pain and joy of life, and the raw hope she harbors for the world, she hopes to touch people with the contents of her soul, even if just momentarily. She is also a passionate vegan and a cat mom.

Author Information

To stay up to date with your favorite writers from this anthology, please check them out on their various writing forums listed below.

Emily Adams-Aucoin

- Instagram   @emilyapoetry

A. Brown

- Instagram   @a_brown_writes

Eloise

- Instagram   @eloise_the_typwriter

Maya Elphick

- Instagram   @m.g.petri

Abbey Forrest

- Instagram   @abbeyforrestpoems
- Facebook   abbeyforrestpoetry
- Twitter   aforrestpoetry
- Blog   www. abbeyforrestpoems.tumbler.com
- Website   www.abbeyforrest.com

M.R.S.

- Instagram   @mrs_poems
- Facebook   morganshortpoetryandphotography
- Blog   www.morganraeshelshort.com

L.M. Steel

- Instagram   @unseen_unheard_poet

Heini Talip

- Instagram   @missfinnpoet

Made in the USA
Lexington, KY
19 November 2018